W9-APB-916

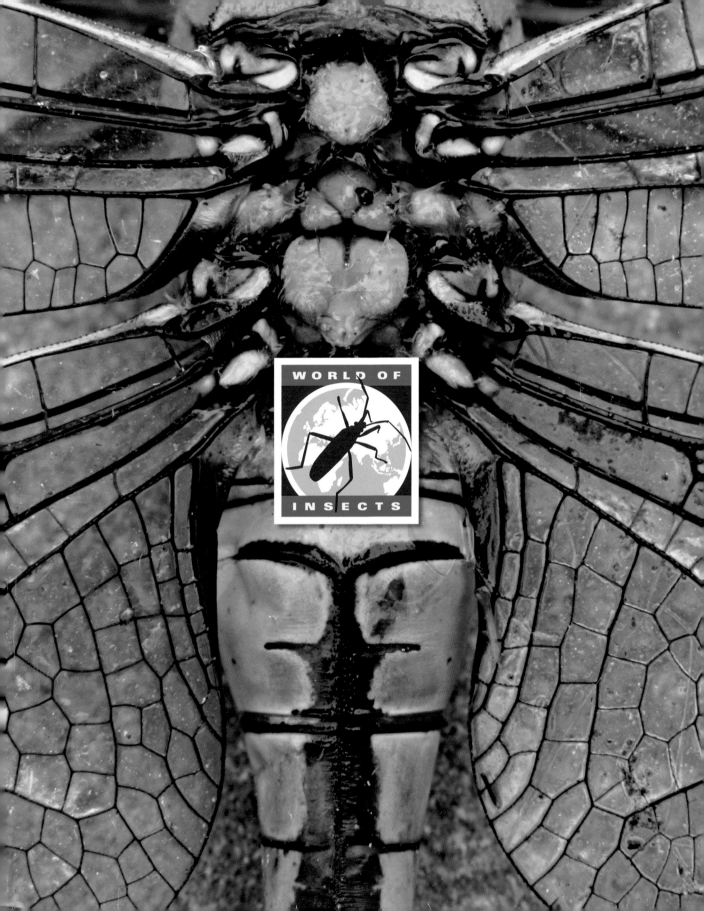

DRAGONFLIES

by Sophie Lockwood

Content Adviser: Michael Breed, Ph.D., Professor,
Ecology and Evolutionary Biology,
The University of Colorado, Boulder

THE CHILD'S WORLD®, MANKATO, MINNESOTA

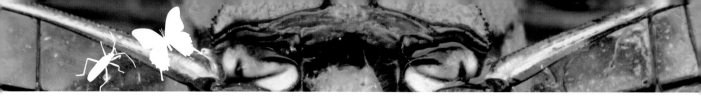

Dragonflies

Published in the United States of America by The Child's World®
1980 Lookout Drive • Mankato, MN 56003-1705
800-599-READ • www.childsworld.com

Acknowledgements:

The Child's World®: Mary Berendes, Publishing Director

The Creative Spark: Mary Francis, Project Director; Wendy Mead, Editor; Deborah Goodsite, Photo Researcher

The Design Lab: Kathleen Petelinsek, Designer, Production Artist, and Cartographer

Photos:

Cover and half title: Herbert Kehrer/zefa/Corbis; frontispiece and CIP: Merlin Farwell/iStockphoto.com

Interior: Alamy: 19 (Tim Gainey); Animals Animals: 5, 22 (Bill Beatty); iStockphoto.com: 5, 10 (Kelly Borsheim), 21 (Johann Frank), 28 (Amanda Rohde), 5, 34 (Sebastien Barrau); Minden Pictures: 33 (Stephen Dalton); David Moskowitz: 8; Oxford Scientific: 25 (Richard Shiell), 36 (Allen Blake Sheldon); SuperStock: 5,14 (age fotostock); Visuals Unlimited: 12 (Charles Melton), 16 (Fritz Polking), 5, 30 (Gary Meszaros).

Map: The Design Lab: 7.

Library of Congress Cataloging-in-Publication Data

Lockwood, Sophie.
  Dragonflies / by Sophie Lockwood.
    p. cm.—(The world of insects)
  Includes index.
  ISBN-13: 978-1-59296-821-3 (library bound: alk. paper)
  ISBN-10: 1-59296-821-X (library bound: alk. paper)
  1. Dragonflies—Juvenile literature. I.Title.
  QL520.L63 2007
  595.7'33—dc22   2006103454

TABLE OF CONTENTS

Chapter One

Migrating Green Darners

The idea of tracking migrating animals may have begun with John James Audubon. Audubon wondered where birds went for the winter and whether they returned each spring. He tied a string to a bird's leg in the fall of 1803 and saw the same bird return in the spring of 1804. Since then, humans have followed the travels of birds, sea turtles, whales, dolphins, butterflies, meerkats, and caribou, among other animals. In the past fifty years, those migrations have been tracked by radio.

Of the four hundred known dragonfly species in North America, which are usually seen around ponds and lakes, nine migrate. Those species include common green darners, wandering gliders, black saddlebags, and blue dashers. For years, scientists wondered where those dragonflies went. No radio transmitter was tiny enough to attach to a dragonfly, so dragonfly migrations could not be tracked until recently.

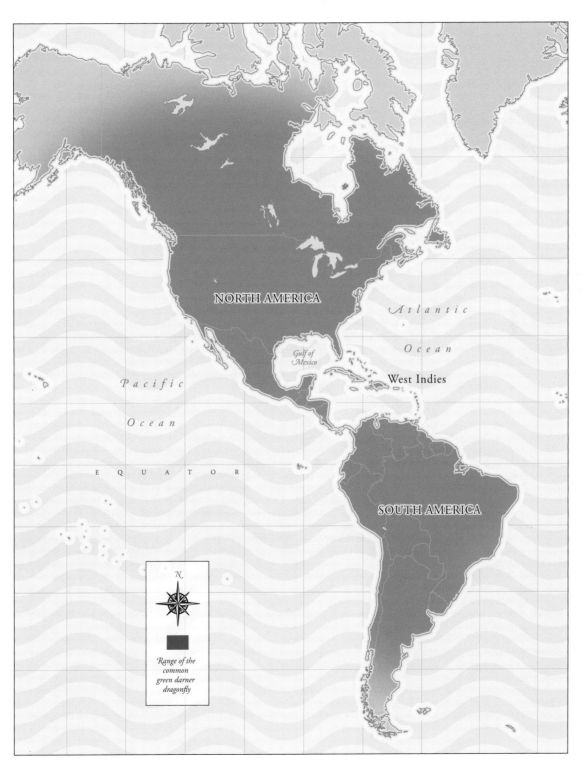

NORTH AMERICA

Atlantic

Ocean

Gulf of
Mexico

West Indies

Pacific

Ocean

E Q U A T O R

SOUTH AMERICA

N

*Range of the
common
green darner
dragonfly*

*The common green darner dragonfly can be found in both
North and South America and in the West Indies.*

The first dragonfly migration tracking followed green darners from the northern United States and southern

A small device put on the underside of a green darner helped scientists follow its every move.

Canada southward. The scientists found that green darners have two populations, a migrating population and a resident population. The migrators travel, and the residents stay home.

The scientists attached miniature transmitters to the bodies of green darner dragonflies and discovered several interesting facts. Traveling by day, the darners follow the same paths as migrating hawks and songbirds. They quickly discovered when they went off course and made accurate course corrections. The dragonflies stopped along the way, resting every three days or so. They also avoided flying in bad weather or when there was a strong wind. After six days, the dragonflies had traveled about 58 kilometers (38 miles) on average.

Darners that arrive in Ontario, Canada, in April have a short time period in which to mate and produce young. The darners mate soon after arriving. The females immediately lay eggs in or near pond or lake water. Nymphs, or young dragonflies, hatch immediately and develop more quickly than the nymphs of resident dragonflies and most other dragonfly species. After just a few months, an adult is ready to emerge and begin its journey south.

In the northern United States or southern Canada, it is easy to tell migrators from residents. On a chilly morning in

April, the nymphs in a pond are residents. The dragonflies buzzing about are migrators that just arrived.

Whether or not they migrate, dragonflies can commonly be found by ponds.

Chapter Two

The Dragonfly Cycle of Life

Dragonflies are common flying insects with bodies designed for swift flying. These creatures zoom around pond and lake areas, searching for prey. Like other insects, they have three main body parts: head, **thorax**, and **abdomen**.

A dragonfly's head has **antennae**, compound eyes, and strong mouthparts. The antennae are short and thin, much like thick eyelashes. Used to smell and feel, the antennae are a dragonfly's main sense organs.

Compound dragonfly eyes have up to 28,000 separate lenses per eye. Called **ommatidia**, these multiple lenses allow dragonflies to see color and motion. They take up most of the insect's head. Because dragonflies are meat eaters, sharp, strong mouthparts are essential. Nymphs have a strong labium, a piercing, tonguelike organ that works like a speargun to catch prey. Adults

have jaws called mandibles strong enough to catch and usually dine on mosquitos, flies, and gnats.

The thorax is the dragonfly's power center. Its strong muscles control two pairs of wings. Catching a dragonfly is not easy because the insect seems able to fly in two different directions at the same time. Of course, that would be impossible, but dragonflies do move swiftly through the air, darting, weaving, and gliding.

The thorax contains a heart, a system of breathing tubes, and six hinged legs. A dragonfly's legs are not

A dragonfly's body has three main sections: head, thorax, and abdomen.

particularly flexible, although they do bend. Generally, dragonflies' legs aren't meant for walking, but for perching and catching prey. The legs have claws at the end to hold onto leaves or twigs. A dragonfly's heart is more like a muscular tube than a human or mammal heart. It pumps **hemolymph**, a yellowish liquid much like plasma in human blood, through the insect's body. The breathing system is called a trachea, and this organ pumps oxygen through the insect's body. During the nymph stage, gills are used to help get oxygen out of the water.

The abdomen contains the digestive, reproductive, and waste-removal organs. The abdomen is ten segments long, with each segment being twice as long as it is wide. Dragonfly digestive organs process proteins, the main nutrient in meat. After nutrients are extracted, the waste passes through the abdomen and is expelled through the anus. Sex organs are also present in the abdomen. Most females have a long, thin **ovipositor** used for laying eggs. Dragonflies must get their nymphs to water, and egg-laying on plants in or near ponds is important.

REPRODUCTION

Dragonflies, unlike butterflies or beetles, have only three steps in their life cycles—

Did You Know?
Dragonfly wings can work independently of each other. Sometimes they beat in a figure-eight pattern, and at other times, they all move together, propelling the dragonfly forward at up to 60 kilometers (35 miles) per hour.

egg, nymph, adult. Adults mate soon after they emerge because they only live a short time as an adult. The male life span is much shorter than the female's. Males generally live from 24 hours to several weeks. Females live longer because they must lay eggs.

A female emperor dragonfly lays her eggs in a pond.

Most males are highly territorial. When a male chooses an area in which he plans to find a mate, it usually has a good egg-laying site. Other dragonflies that enter the male's territory will be dive-bombed and forced to move away. Male skimmers select a perch over their territory and keep a watchful eye out for invaders. Hawkers and emeralds choose to fly around and around, driving away intruders by showing greater flying skills or by being larger. On occasion, dragonflies—small and fragile as they appear—can become violent when protecting a territory.

Females of different species lay their eggs in different ways. Some use their ovipositors to place eggs individually inside leaves or stems. Others lay a raft of eggs at a time or lay their eggs directly in the water. For some, the eggs are protected by the plant. For others, the eggs lie under a jellylike coating. Typically, a female lays from 500 to 1,500 eggs. That number also depends on the species doing the egg-laying. Eggs hatch from 5 to 60 days after being laid. The time from laying to hatching depends on the temperature and location of the eggs.

Very few eggs survive to adulthood because so many things can go wrong. The weather can be too wet or too dry. Temperatures can be too high or too low. Predators can feed on the eggs or the nymphs.

When it hatches, a nymph emerges from the egg and begins its most important job—eating. Nymphs are carnivores. They begin feeding on water fleas, worms, and eggs

A group of four-spotted chaser dragonflies lay their eggs.

of other insects and fish. The nymph's **exoskeleton**, or outer shell, is hard, like a fingernail, and must be discarded as the nymph grows. This process is called molting, and a nymph may molt from 8 to 18 times during this stage of life. A nymph lives underwater until it is ready to emerge as an adult. This can take from a few months to several years.

As the nymph grows, the size of the creatures it eats increases. The nymph lies in wait for snails, water beetles, caddis fly nymphs, or any other small, freshwater critter. It strikes with its labium—the sharp, tonguelike part of its mouth—to catch its prey.

When it is time for the nymph to become an adult, body changes occur that put the dragonfly in great danger. The gills stop working, and the nymph must breathe air. It climbs up a reed or stem and places the top half of its body above water.

Emergence, the process of leaving the nymph body and becoming an adult, usually takes place during the night or just before dawn. The nymph's exoskeleton cracks, and the adult dragonfly slowly pulls itself out of the shell. The process is exhausting, taking two or more hours. Then, the dragonfly pumps fluid into its wings until they harden. Then, the fluid is drained from the wings and pumped into the abdomen until the dragonfly's outer shell hardens.

While this is taking place, birds, toads, lizards, and even raindrops present a danger to the dragonfly. During this stage, called the teneral stage, dragonflies cannot yet fly, nor can they escape underwater. They become easy meals for predators. As for the raindrops, a single drop can damage an unformed wing permanently, and dragonflies must fly to survive.

PREDATORS

As with every other insect, dragonflies have their share of predators. In the egg stage, they feed fish, toads, lizards, ducks, geese, and other waterbirds. As adults, they are a challenge for birds to catch in flight.

Some birds specialize in preying on adult dragonflies. The northern hobby, a smallish falcon, is a fast flyer and can swoop down on dragonflies at great speed. Sparrow hawks, falcons, and jacamars also feast on dragonflies. One surprising predator is the purple martin. Only 17 to 20 centimeters (7 to 8 inches) long from beak to tail feathers, purple martins feast on large insects. Some of the dragonflies a purple martin eats are half the bird's overall length.

Another group of predators that feed on dragonflies is other insects. Robber flies and wasps prey on adult dragonflies. Many dragonfly species will eat the eggs, nymphs, and adult dragonflies of another species.

When a dragonfly emerges from its shell, it pumps fluid through its body to expand its wings.

Chapter Three

Dragonflies and More Dragonflies

The earth was a very different place 250 million years ago. Fish, coral, and other creatures dominated the seas but were dying out, while many insect species survived. Among those insects were giant dragonflies with wingspans measuring 1 meter (3.28 feet) across.

Today's dragonflies are smaller, with a maximum body length of 15 centimeters (6 inches) and a maximum wingspan of 19 centimeters (7.5 inches). Of course, many dragonflies and damselflies worldwide are much smaller than that.

Telling a dragonfly from a damselfly is not always easy—they look very much alike. One way to do so is to look at the body shape. Dragonflies have shorter, chubbier abdomens. The rear wings of dragonflies tend to be larger than the front wings, and dragonflies rest with their wings spread open. Damselflies perch with their wings placed together over their backs.

Most dragonflies fly by day, although some are active at dawn or dusk. At night, they roost on branches, shrubs, or tree bark. Many dragonflies may roost together in a tight cluster.

Because dragonflies need to eat 10 to 20 percent of their own body weight daily, they spend the daytime hunting for prey.

Would You Believe?
The largest living dragonfly is the giant petaltail (*Petalura ingentissima*) from northeastern Australia. The giant petaltail has a wingspan of approximately 160 millimeters (6.3 inches).

You're most likely to see a dragonfly going by during the daytime.

Catching insects in midair is called hawking. Hovering over plant life to seize small insects is called gleaning. Dragonflies eat

A dragonfly makes a meal of a fly.

a wide variety of insects, including flies, moths, butterflies, mosquitoes, and even hummingbirds.

Many people have noticed that catching a dragonfly is not an easy task. This is because a dragonfly's flight pattern is unique. The base of the wings are jointed at the thorax so that one pair of wings can thrust downward while the other thrusts upward. To increase speed and avoid predators, dragonflies can make all four wings work together, thrusting in the same direction at the same time.

Dragonflies and butterflies share one similar type of behavior—hilltopping. The insects swarm together on the top of a hill, far from open water. Scientists are not sure why they do this, but it is possible that this is a type of dating. The dragonflies might be looking for mates.

MAJOR DRAGONFLY GROUPS

Dragonfly species are classified into larger groups, or families. Each family group shares some similar characteristics, such as size, shape, coloring, or habitat. Petaltails, for example, belong to an ancient family of dragonflies that lives in countries surrounding the Pacific Ocean. Most live close to bogs, swamps, or seeps and lay their eggs on moss.

Dragonflies Around the World
Because dragonflies spend so much time around water, some cultures have given the dragonfly water-based nicknames.
 Germany: water peacock
 Netherlands: water nymph
 France: water spirit
 Italy: keeper of the fish, guard of the tubs

Goldenrings all bear similar body markings. They have black abdomens with gold rings and are known to lay their eggs in sand or gravel in mountain streambeds. Goldenrings are found in North America, Central America, Asia, Europe, and North Africa.

One of the largest families of dragonflies is Libellulidae (ly-bell-LOO-lih-dee), better known as chasers, skimmers, and darters. More than 1,000 dragonfly species belong to this family.

Emeralds go by the scientific name Corduliidae (cor-DOO-lee-ih-dee). Their eyes, as their name implies, are a brilliant green, and their abdomens are metallic green or black. Another group of green dragonflies are the river

The North American Dragonfly Time Line

Spring	Common green darner, springtime darner, common baskettail, lancet clubtail, emerald spreadwing, eastern forktail, common whitetail
Early Summer	Familiar bluet, ebony jewelwing, twin-spotted spiketail, black-shouldered spinyleg, Illinois River cruiser, slaty skimmer, prince baskettail
Summer	Blue dasher, eastern pondhawk, calico pennant, Halloween pennant, widow skimmer, fawn darner
Early Fall	Black saddlebags, shadow darner, wandering glider, spot-winged glider

emeralds. River emeralds, too, have metallic green bodies. They also have spidery legs and lay their eggs by skimming over water to wash them off the lower abdomen.

The red skimmer is a member of the Libellulidae family.

Hine's Emerald Dragonfly

The Hine's emerald dragonfly is one of the few insects found on the endangered species list. It is a small, delicate green dragonfly with yellow stripes on its sides. Although the Hine's emerald used to be fairly widespread in the Midwest, today it is limited to Illinois, Michigan, Missouri, and Wisconsin.

The Hine's emerald prefers spring-fed marshes, and the water in these marches usually has high levels of calcium carbonate from underlying limestone. This type of habitat is in serious danger. To create more farmland or housing, engineers fill in or drain wetland habitats. Loss of habitat endangers the Hine's emerald dragonfly's survival. **Pollution** in remaining wetlands and in groundwater also affect the survival of this species.

To save the Hine's emerald dragonfly, the United States Fish and Wildlife Service has placed this insect on its endangered species list. Scientists are studying other ways to ensure the species' survival, including breeding these dragonflies in zoos or laboratories and establishing protected wetland environments.

Chapter Four

In Appreciation of Dragonflies

Dragonflies sew together the fingers and toes of sleeping people. They sew together the lips of scolding mothers, rude children, and cursing men. These statements may seem ridiculous today, but people used to believe them. In the Middle Ages, many Europeans thought that dragonflies were associated with the devil and called them "devil's needles."

Other cultures also had odd names for dragonflies. In the United States, some people called them "mosquito hawks" or "darning needles." Dragonflies have been called "snake doctors" and "snake feeders." Regardless of the names used, they commonly flit around lakes and ponds for the delight of all.

ADMIRED IN JAPAN

The Japanese consider dragonflies a sign of good luck. The insect is a symbol

Who Said That?
Crimson pepper pod
add two pairs of wings, and look
darting dragonfly
—Basho (1644–94), Japanese
  haiku master

of courage, strength, and victory in that country. For centuries, the Japanese believed that if a dragonfly flew into a person's home, it was a visit from the spirit of a dead friend or relative.

Considered the most indestructible of insects, the dragonfly is the emblem of Japan. Japanese artists regularly

These ancient insects have been admired by many cultures for hundreds of years.

portray dragonflies in landscapes, on pottery, and in jewelry. Poets have written numerous haiku and other poems with dragonflies as the topic.

FEARED IN EUROPE

For centuries, Europeans were not quite so kind to dragonflies. Most felt dragonflies were a threat to life or good health. They were connected to devils and carried on the devils' wishes among people.

Long ago in Sweden, when a dragonfly flew around a person's head, some believed that person was in serious trouble. There was a weight on that person's soul. Of course, weight on the soul meant trouble was on the way. That trouble could be anything. When the person in question fell sick, died, or lost something of value, that problem was considered foretold by the dragonfly's visit.

Not all European cultures saw the dragonfly as evil. The Norse goddess Freya was the goddess of love. Linked to dragonflies, Freya was a symbol of romance and joy.

Would You Believe?
More than 2,600 years ago, the emperor of Japan nicknamed that nation Akitsu shima (ah-KEET-soo SHE-mah), Island of the Dragonfly.

29

The beauty and grace of the dragonflies, such as these calico pennants, have inspired Native American artists.

NATIVE AMERICANS AND DRAGONFLIES

Many Native American cultures have legends or tales regarding dragonflies. The Navajo saw dragonflies as flighty and carefree and included them in a creation myth. According to the Navajo, the dragonfly was one of the twelve original "people," along with dark ants, red ants, yellow beetles, and other common insects. These "people" came to life at a place the Navajo called the House Made of Red Rock. It was from these important insects that all life evolved. Today, Navajos often show dragonflies in sand paintings, a traditional and unique art form.

The rock art of the Hopi often pictures dragonflies. In these works, the dragonfly is depicted as one long vertical line crossed by two shorter horizontal lines at the top. The Hopi perform rituals in a room called a kiva, and many kiva walls feature murals with dragonflies.

The Zuni connected dragonflies with the success of their corn crops. Black, white, and red dragonflies arrived in the area when corn tassels bloom. This was a good omen—the crop would thrive, and so would the Zuni, who depended on corn as a regular part of their diet.

Did You Know?
The artist Louis Comfort Tiffany frequently created stained glass lamps with a dragonfly motif.

Chapter Five

Man and Dragonflies

In a rice paddy in Thailand, mosquitoes breed by the millions. Using chemicals to kill the mosquitoes is not possible. The chemicals would poison the rice. Fed up with swarms of biting mosquitoes, farmers discovered a solution. This solution came in the form of another flying insect, the dragonfly.

While the dragonflies—either as nymphs or adults—do not completely eliminate mosquitoes, they do reduce mosquito populations by about 90 percent. Dragonflies also feed on flies and midges, while dragonfly nymphs provide pest control by devouring insect larvae and tadpoles.

One adult dragonfly can consume hundreds of flying insects in a day. In areas where flying insects carry diseases, such as dengue (DEHNG-ghee) fever or malaria, dragonflies can be used to reduce the spread of disease. In Myanmar during the 1980s, an outbreak of dengue fever spread

rapidly. The mosquitoes carrying the disease bred in the water jars that held a family's water supply. Scientists suggested

A dragonfly nymph takes a bite out of a stickleback fish.

placing dragonfly nymphs in the water, and the nymphs took care of the problem by eating mosquito larvae and thereby reducing the mosquito population.

A BALANCE IN NATURE

Scientists consider dragonflies to be **indicator species**. In midsummer, a pond with no dragonflies is a very

Dragonflies, such as this Halloween pendant skipper, help scientists learn whether a habitat is healthy.

sick body of water. Water pollution may come in several different forms. The pollution may kill all fish, insects, mammals, and plants around a body of water. It also might encourage plant growth to the extent that the plants choke the life from the pond. The plants could cover the entire pond, preventing sunlight from penetrating the water and reducing water oxygen levels. Animals that live in the water would not survive, and that includes dragonfly nymphs.

While it may seem to be a minor thing, the loss of dragonflies to a lake, pond, or river tells a sad story. Nature is a balancing act. Dragonflies are both prey and predators. Many insects and other animals feed on plants and produce eggs, larvae, and young. Dragonfly nymphs, along with other animals, feed on those eggs, larvae, and young and control populations of other small pond-dwellers, such as mosquitos and gnats. Dragonflies play a key role in preserving the balance of nature. As adults, they feed on flying insects that swarm around the pond.

When dragonflies leave a pond, it is because they cannot live, and the balance of nature is thrown off. Populations of critters that nymph and adult dragonflies eat explode. Animals that normally feed on nymphs and adult dragonflies must go elsewhere for a meal.

Many wetlands are being destroyed so that new houses can be built.

THE HUMAN IMPACT

Humans play an important role in the success and survival of dragonflies. We fill in wetlands where dragonflies mate and lay their eggs. We pollute the waters that dragonflies need for their nymphs to thrive.

Wetlands can be permanent—marshes, fens, bogs, and swamps. They can be temporary, such as prairie potholes. For centuries, humans have filled in or drained wetlands to create usable land. They use that land for farms, factories, or housing developments. In doing so, humans destroy habitats for hundreds of animal and plant species, including the dragonfly.

Pollution poisons our air, water, and land. The effects of pollution on dragonflies are dramatic and should be a warning sign to humans. When the water or air is not fit for dragonflies, humans should not want to drink that water or breathe that air.

Dragonflies, like all insects, come in a large number of species and have an enormous population. It would seem that losing one or two species would not matter much. However, if that lost species is one that used to thrive where your water comes from, you might feel that loss is too great. It would certainly be something to think about.

Glossary

abdomen (AB-doh-men) elongated portion of the body of an arthropod, located behind the thorax

antennae (an-TEN-nee) thin, sensory organs found on the heads of many insects

emergence (ee-MUR-jehnse) in the dragonfly world, the act of escaping from the exoskeleton and coming out as an adult

exoskeleton (ek-soh-SKELL-eh-tun) hard outer shell found on animals such as lobsters, ants, and dragonflies

hemolymph (HEE-moh-limf) a fluid in an insect's body that carries nutrients

indicator species (IN-dih-cay-tuhr SPEE-sheez) animal or plant that tells scientists whether an environment is healthy or polluted

ommatidia (ahm-uh-TIH-dee-uh) the visual facets, or lenses, of an insect eye

ovipositor (oh-vih-PAHZ-ih-tur) a tubular organ at the end of the abdomen of female insects and other species, used for laying eggs

pollution (poh-LOO-shun) chemicals or other matter that taints air, land, or water

thorax (THOR-aks) the body section of an insect, crustacean, or spider

For More Information

Watch It

Common Dragonflies and Damselflies of Eastern North America, DVD. (Hillsborough, NC: Brownbag Productions, 2004.)

Life in the Undergrowth, DVD. (Burbank, CA.: BBC, 2006.)

Wonder of Nature in Our Backyard, DVD. (Atlanta: Marshall Fairman Productions, 2002.)

Read It

Berger, Cynthia. *Dragonflies.* Mechanicsburg, PA: Stackpole Books, 2004.

Brooks, Steve. *Dragonflies.* London: The Natural History Museum, 2003.

Kuhn, Dwight. *Dragonflies and Damselflies.* Farmington Hills, MI: Blackbirch Press, 2005.

McEvey, Shane F. *Dragonflies (Insects and Spiders).* Broomall, PA: Chelsea House Publications, 2001.

Merrick, Patrick. *Dragonflies.* Chanhassen, MN: The Child's World, 2006.

Pringle, Laurence. *Dragon in the Sky.* New York: Scholastic, 2001.

Look It Up

Visit our Web site for lots of links about dragonflies:
http://www.childsworld.com/links

Note to Parents, Teachers, and Librarians: We routinely verify our Web links to make sure they are safe, active sites—so encourage your readers to check them out!

The Animal Kingdom
Where Do Dragonflies Fit In?

Kingdom: Animal

Phylum: Arthropoda

Class: Insecta

Order: Odonata

Genus and Species: 5,200–6,500 species

Index

About the Author
Sophie Lockwood is a former teacher and a longtime writer. She writes textbooks, newspaper articles, and magazine articles. Sophie enjoys writing about animals and their habits. The most interesting part of her research, Sophie says, is learning how scientists apply their knowledge to save endangered species. She lives with her husband in the foothills of the Blue Ridge Mountains.